NIGHT SKY STORIES

THE STORY OF
ORION
A ROMAN CONSTELLATION MYTH

A RETELLING BY
THOMAS KINGSLEY TROUPE

ILLUSTRATED BY
GERALD GUERLAIS

PICTURE WINDOW BOOKS
a capstone imprint

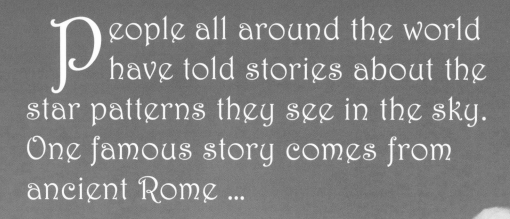

People all around the world have told stories about the star patterns they see in the sky. One famous story comes from ancient Rome ...

Long ago there lived a mighty man named Orion. He was the son of Neptune, god of the sea. Orion was a great hunter. With his bow and arrows, and his club and shield, there was nothing Orion couldn't hunt.

Orion's hunting stories spread throughout the land. He was quick to boast. "I could kill every animal on Earth!"

4

Hearing such things angered the gods. They thought Orion should respect all living creatures. But because Orion was Neptune's son, the gods did nothing.

Diana, goddess of the moon, pulled the moon across the sky each night. One evening, she spied Orion hunting in the woods below. Diana also loved to hunt, and she wished to meet Orion. She went down to Earth and hunted with him.

As time went by, Diana often forgot her duties as moon goddess. She spent all of her time with Orion. The two of them had fallen in love.

Apollo, god of the sun and Diana's twin brother, watched Diana and Orion from the sky. He grew angry. With Diana busy, Apollo was left to pull both the sun and the moon across the sky. If he got rid of Orion, Diana would come back.

One day Apollo spied a familiar shape out in the sea. "Do you see that shiny rock far off in the water, sister?" he asked. "I doubt you could strike it with an arrow."

Diana placed an arrow in her bowstring and let it go. Her aim was true.

Diana's arrow flew across the water and struck the rock. But it was no rock. It was Orion swimming in the sea! When Diana saw him struggling in the water, she realized what she had done. But it was too late—the arrow killed Orion.

Hoping to save him, Diana brought Orion's body to Ophiuchus. The medicine man made a potion that brought Orion back to life.

Diana and Orion were overjoyed. But some of the gods were not so happy.

Pluto, the god of the underworld, had been waiting for Orion to arrive. Pluto felt cheated when Orion returned to life.

Jupiter wanted to help Pluto. But he knew Neptune would be angry if he harmed Orion. He decided to punish Ophiuchus by unleashing a powerful lightning bolt. The bolt struck Ophiuchus and killed him.

Apollo was also angry when he learned Orion
had survived. He called for the monster Scorpio.
He ordered the scorpion to attack Orion.

Scorpio quickly crept up on Orion's hunting path.

Orion saw the scorpion approaching. "A mere bug?" he cried. "Fighting you is hardly worth my sweat!"

Scorpio attacked. The battle raged, and Scorpio proved to be a difficult enemy.

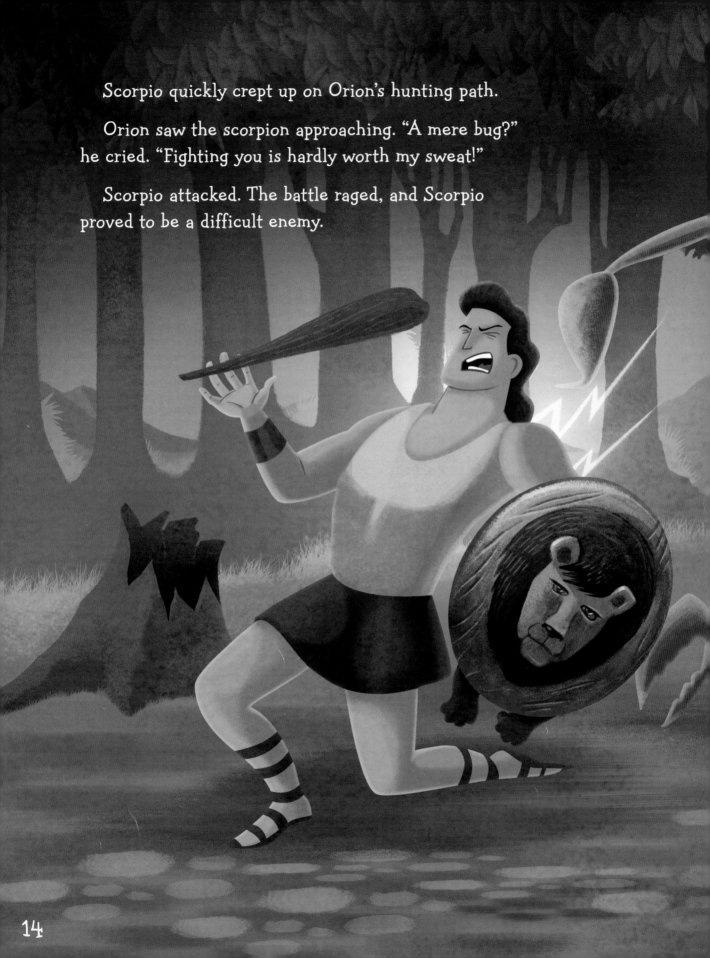

"I'm wasting my time with you!" Orion finally said. Then he made a final mistake—he turned his back on the scorpion.

Scorpio quickly struck. Poison coursed through Orion's body. In minutes, he fell to the ground, dead.

Diana found Orion's body. She knew it was Scorpio's sting that had killed him. She set out for revenge.

When she tracked down the scorpion, Diana readied her bow. "You have taken my beloved Orion from me!" she shouted. "Now taste my arrow!"

With a single strike, Scorpio was dead. With Orion's death avenged, Diana raced back to her beloved's side.

Diana brought Orion once again to the medicine man's home. She found the house empty. A neighbor told her of Ophiuchus' fate.

With no other choice, Diana pleaded with the gods to save Orion. But the gods were silent.

From the sky, Apollo saw his sister's sadness. He felt sorry for her. To ease her pain, he helped Diana raise Orion to the winter sky. They turned him into stars, so Diana could see Orion every night.

Later Apollo placed Scorpio in the summer sky. There the giant scorpion would never be able to battle Orion again.

LEARN MORE

For as long as people have lived, stories have been told about the constellations. In the northern hemisphere, Orion can be seen in the winter night sky. Seven bright stars form his hourglass shape. Three stars in a row form his bright belt. He carries his club and shield, continuing to hunt.

Scorpio is in the summer sky. He appears as Orion disappears. The giant scorpion is a reminder to Orion, and everyone, to respect all of earth's creatures.

In Hindu myth, Orion's constellation is actually the god Prajapati, who became a deer. The three stars of Orion's belt represent an arrow piercing the god. So, in Hindu myth, the tables are turned. The hunter has become the hunted.

CAST OF CHARACTERS

Orion—a mighty hunter; Neptune's son

Neptune—god of the sea; father to Orion

Diana—goddess of the moon and of hunting; sister to Apollo

Apollo—god of the sun and of music and healing; brother to Diana

Ophiuchus—a medicine man

Pluto—king of the underworld and god of riches

Jupiter—god of the sky and thunder and king of the gods

Scorpio—a scorpion monster

GLOSSARY

boast—to brag and act as if better than others

constellation—a group of stars that forms a shape

fate—the outcome of a situation

myth—a story told in ancient times; a myth often tried to explain natural events

potion—a mixture of liquids thought to have magical effects

scorpion—an arachnid with a long body and a jointed tail tipped with a poisonous stinger

READ MORE

Forest, Christopher. *The Kids' Guide to the Constellations.* Kids' Guides. Mankato, Minn.: Capstone Press, 2012.

Kim, F. S. *Constellations.* A True Book. New York: Children's Press, 2010.

Peters, Stephanie True. *Orion.* The Library of Constellations. New York: PowerKids Press, 2003.

INTERNET SITES

FactHound offers a safe, fun way to find Internet sites related to this book. All of the sites on FactHound have been researched by our staff.

Here's all you do:

Visit *www.facthound.com*

Type in this code: 9781404873773

Super-cool stuff! Check out projects, games and lots more at **www.capstonekids.com**

Thanks to our advisers for their expertise, research, and advice:
David Burgess
District #77 Planetarium Director, Mankato

Terry Flaherty, PhD, Professor of English
Minnesota State University, Mankato

Editor: Shelly Lyons
Designer: Alison Thiele
Art Director: Nathan Gassman
Production Specialist: Danielle Ceminsky
The illustrations in this book were created digitally.

Picture Window Books
1710 Roe Crest Drive
North Mankato, Minnesota 56003
877-845-8392
www.capstonepub.com

Library of Congress Cataloging-in-Publication Data
Troupe, Thomas Kingsley.
The story of Orion : a Roman constellation myth : a retelling / by Thomas Kingsley Troupe ; illustrations by Gerald Guerlais.
p. cm. — (Capstone picture window books. Night sky stories)
Includes index.
ISBN 978-1-4048-7377-3 (library binding)
ISBN 978-1-4048-7718-4 (paperback)
ISBN 978-1-4048-7989-8 (ebook PDF)
1. Orion (Greek mythology)—Juvenile literature.
2. Mythology, Roman—Juvenile literature. 3. Mythology, Greek—Juvenile literature. 4. Orion (Constellation)—Juvenile literature. 5. Constellations—Juvenile literature
I. Guerlais, Gerald. II. Title.
BL820.O65T76 2013
292.1'3—dc23   2012001006

Printed in the United States of America in North Mankato, Minnesota.
042012   006682CGF12